THE WINKING, BLINKING SEA

To Priscilla
For many years of loving friendship and
for sparking my interest in the wonders of the sea

ACKNOWLEDGMENT

I am most grateful to the following for sharing their research with me: Dr. Margo G. Haygood, Assistant Professor of Marine Biology, Scripps Institution of Oceanography, University of California, San Diego; Dr. Bruce H. Robinson, Senior Scientist and Chairman of the Science Department, Monterey Bay Aquarium Research Institute; Dr. Jeff Seigel, Curator of Fishes, Los Angeles County Museum of Natural History; Dr. Rocky Strong, University of California, Santa Barbara; Dr. James G. Morin, Director of the Shoals Marine Laboratory, Cornell University; and Dr. Edith Widder, Senior Scientist and Director, Bioluminescent Department, Harbor Branch Oceanographic Institution.

Photographs courtesy of © Dave Haas/Bruce Coleman, Inc.: cover; The National Audubon Society Collection/Photo Researchers, Inc.: pp. 4-5 (© George Lower), 8-9 (© Richard Rowan); © 1999/Youngbluth/Harbor Branch Oceanographic Institution, Inc.: p. 7; Science Source/Photo Researchers, Inc.: pp. 8 (left), 11 (© M. I. Walker); Marty Snyderman: p. 12; © 1999 Norbert Wu/www.norbertwu.com: pp. 15, 20 (bottom left), 24, 27, 28-29; Tom Stack & Associates: pp. 16 (© Randy Morse), 17 (© Dave B. Fleetham); Animals Animals: pp. 18-19 (© Dale Sarver), 32 (© Herb Segars); Peter Girguis: pp. 20 (top left), 23, 31; Bill Curtsinger/NGS Image Collection: p. 20 (right)

Published by The Millbrook Press, Inc.
2 Old New Milford Road, Brookfield, CT 06804   www.millbrookpress.com

Library of Congress Cataloging-in-Publication Data
Batten, Mary.
The winking, blinking sea : all about bioluminescence / Mary Batten.
p. cm.
Summary: Explains bioluminescence in ocean life, giving examples of sea creatures that glow, such as ostracods, Bermuda fire worms, and flashlight fish.
ISBN 0-7613-1550-0 (lib. bdg.)
1. bioluminescence—Juvenile literature. [1. Bioluminescence.] I. Title.
QH641 .B38   2000   571'.4358—dc21   99-048391

THE WINKING, BLINKING SEA

ALL ABOUT BIOLUMINESCENCE

MARY BATTEN

The Millbrook Press   Brookfield, Connecticut

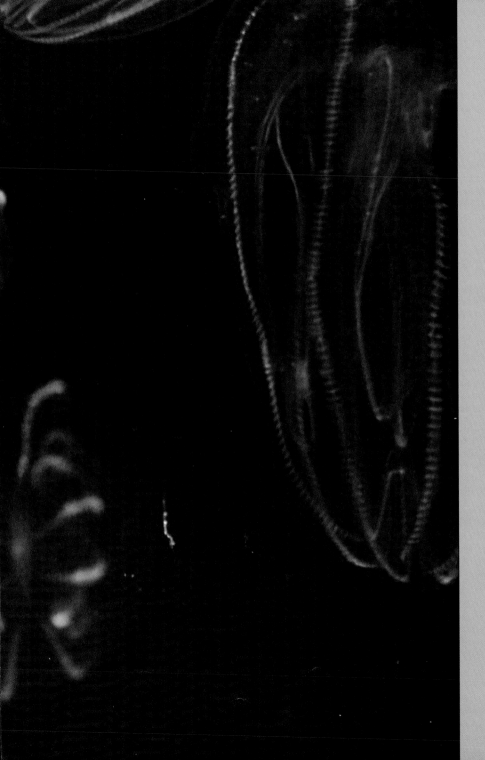

When the sun sets and darkness falls over the land, millions of tiny lights twinkle under the sea like distant stars in a watery galaxy. These are not electric lights made by a hot current of electricity flowing through wires. Sea lights are cold lights that some ocean animals make from chemicals inside their bodies. Scientists call this light bioluminescence (bi-o-loo-mi-NEH-sens). *Bio* means "life," and *lumin* means "light." So *bioluminescence* means "living light." Animals that make living light are called bioluminescent. There are not many bioluminescent animals on land, but the sea is full of them.

IF YOU LET YOUR IMAGINATION GO, THESE BIOLUMINESCENT JELLYFISH LOOK LIKE GALAXIES.

Like fireflies on land, animals in the sea use their lights to help them survive. Some flash a special signal that tells who they are. Some glow with color to attract mates. Some use their lights to scare enemies. Some use their lights to find food. Some hide in glittering bursts of miniature fireworks.

A SIPHONOPHORE AND ITS AMAZING ARRAY OF TENTACLES

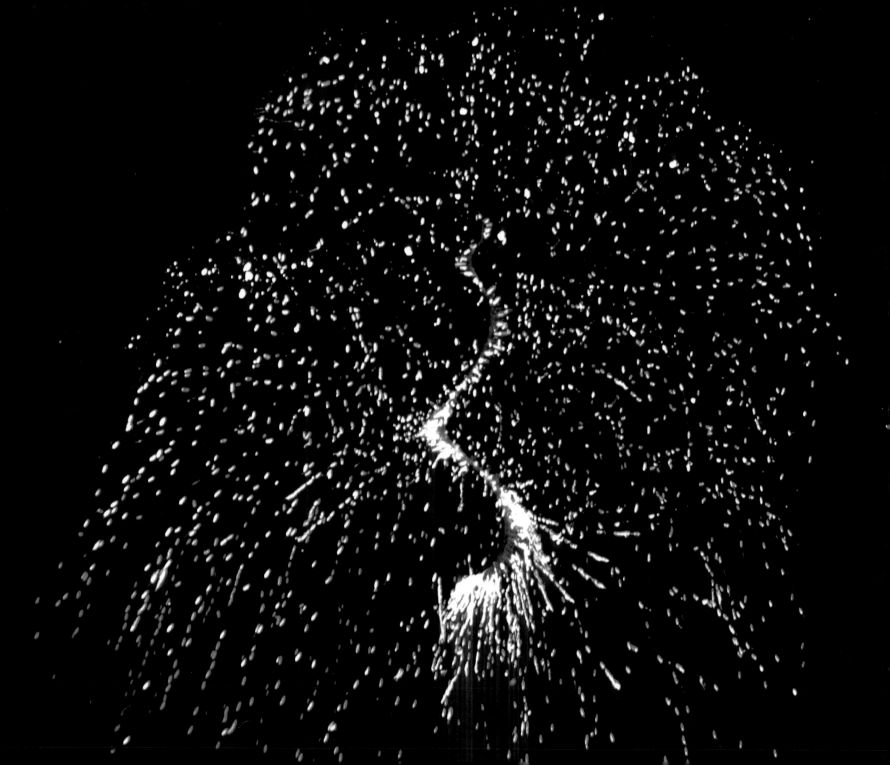

If you have ever taken a boat ride on the ocean at night, you may have seen a silvery greenish glow as the bow cut through the water. This glow is made by millions of living things called dinoflagellates (di-no-FLA-jel-lates). One dinoflagellate is about the size of a pencil point. The

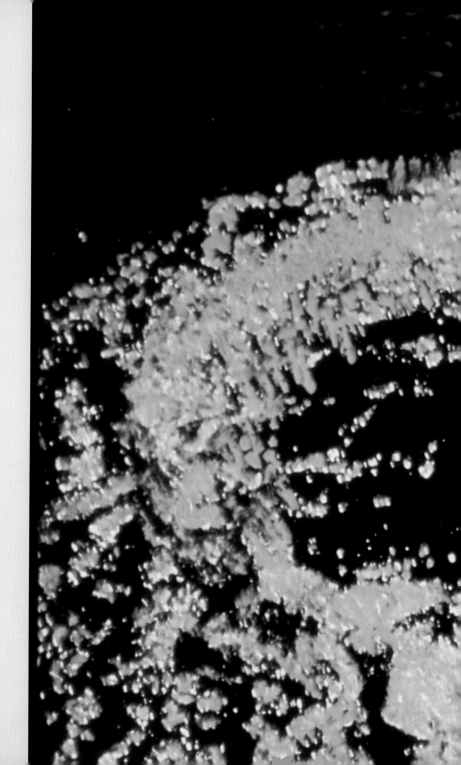

ONE DINOFLAGELLATE ...

light of millions together can be seen when anything—a boat, or even a bubble—disturbs them.

Divers entering the water collide with hundreds of thousands of these tiny bioluminescent organisms, causing them to glow. With dive lights turned off, divers' bodies are outlined in eerie bioluminescent glitter.

... AND THE EFFECT OF MILLIONS.

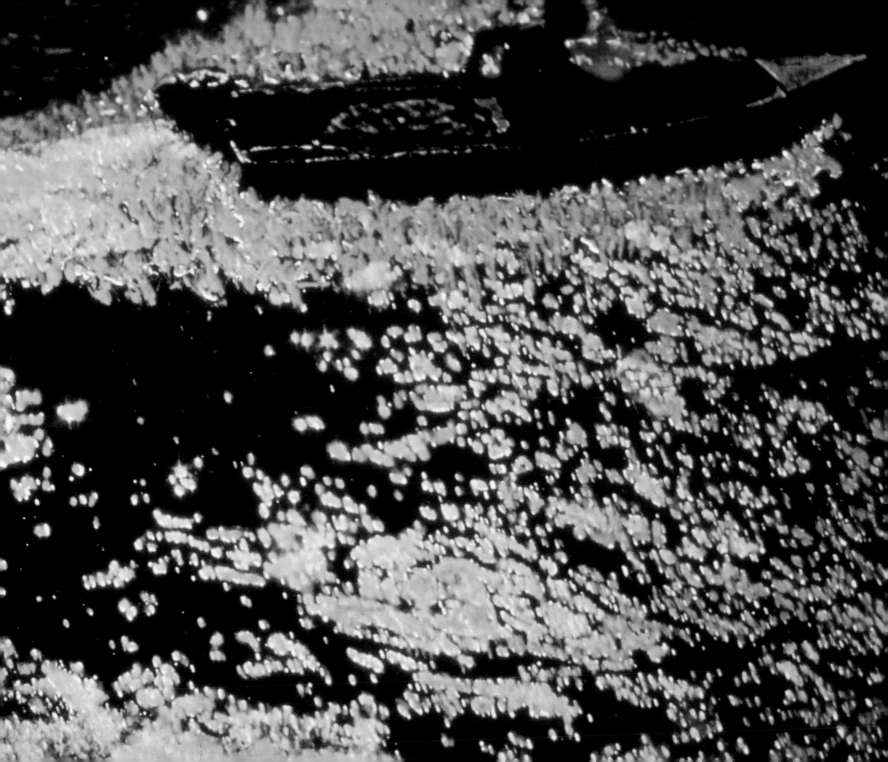

Every night about an hour after sunset in the warm, shallow waters above Caribbean coral reefs, thousands of tiny, brilliant blue lights blink on. These lights are made by male ostracods, little shellfish no bigger than sesame seeds. The males swim around, releasing flowing droplets from glands in their upper lips. Each male leaves a trail of glowing spots. Some glow for ten or fifteen seconds; others glow for less than one-tenth of a second. Some flash like Christmas tree lights. Male ostracods flash their blue lights to attract females.

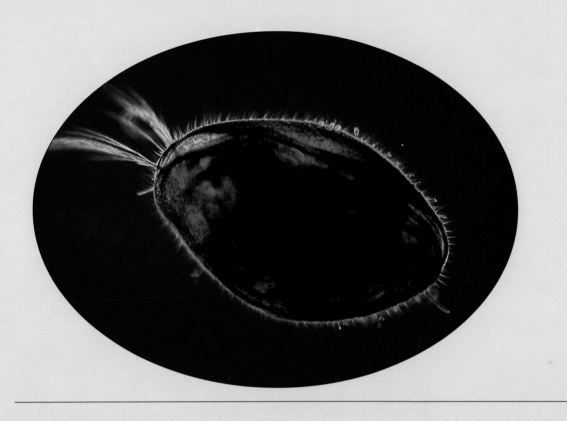

A TINY OSTRACOD

The fire worm flashes a green light. Half an inch long, the fire worm is a giant next to the ostracod. Fire worms are found throughout the world's oceans. Like ostracods, they use their light for mating. When female fire worms are ready to mate, they swim along the water's surface. Their bodies glow, and they slowly release an emerald-green spew to attract males. Males swim as fast as they can toward the females, flashing their own green body light. When males and females meet, they continue glowing, releasing their sperm and eggs together in a brilliant green spiral.

A FIRE WORM AT REST ON A SEA FAN

The flashlight fish doesn't make its own light. It depends on its partners—bioluminescent bacteria that live in the fish's light organ.

The light organ, which is the size of a kidney bean, is home to about a billion bacteria that glow all the time.

The flashlight fish switches its light on and off with a kind of eyelid that covers the light organ. Flashlight fishes live in warm, tropical oceans throughout the world, but they are difficult to find because they hide in underwater caves until it is completely dark.

On nights when there is no moon they swim out and use their light organ to hunt for food.

THE LIGHT ORGAN IS THAT WHITE PATCH RIGHT UNDERNEATH THE FLASHLIGHT FISH'S EYE.

Squids are the special-effects artists of the sea. Their skin contains pigment cells called chromatophores (kro-MAT-o-fors) that enable squids to change colors and patterns in a fraction of a second. Bioluminescent bacteria living on the squid's skin or in special body pouches add to the lightning-fast changes.

A CLOSE-UP OF A SQUID'S FIN REVEALS RAINBOW BURSTS OF BIOLUMINESCENCE.

False eyespots, zebra stripes, silver sides, or glittering eyebrows appear, giving the squid many fantastic disguises. One second the animal is silver; the next, black and invisible.

Some deep-sea squids trick their enemies by suddenly disappearing in a cloud of bluish-green light. Squids make this light screen by squirting light-making chemicals into the water. Hidden by the glow, the squids make their getaway.

THIS SQUID TRIES TO BURY ITSELF WHEN DANGER—IN THE FORM OF THE CAMERAPERSON—APPEARS, BUT THE BIOLUMINESCENT GLOW REMAINS.

LOOKING UP FROM UNDERNEATH A PORICTHYS,
YOU CAN SEE THE TINY LIGHTS ON ITS BELLY.

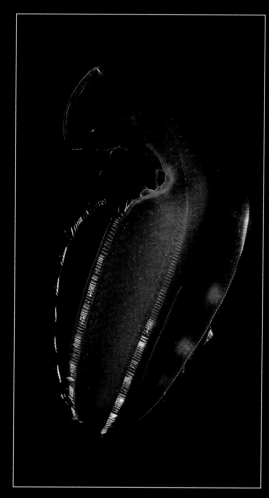

A CTENOPHORE, AN ORGANISM THAT IS
LITTLE MORE THAN A STOMACH WITH A
MOUTH (BUT WHICH IS NOT A JELLYFISH),
DISPLAYS BEAUTIFUL STRIPES OF LIGHT.

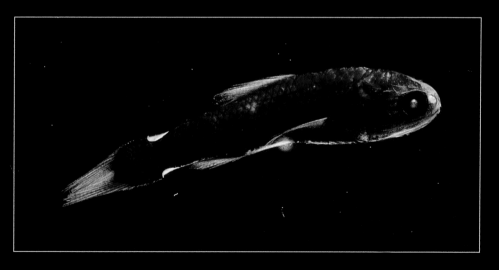

THIS LANTERN FISH HAS LIGHTS ON ITS BELLY, AS WELL AS TWO LIGHT SPOTS
ON ITS TAIL, WHICH LOOK LIKE EYES AND CONFUSE ITS ENEMIES.

Thousands of feet below the surface of the ocean, it is always dark, like outer space. No sunlight reaches this hidden world. The only light that animals have is the light they make themselves. Only scientists traveling in small submarines that can plunge more than half a mile down have seen these animals.

Many deep-sea fishes have lights on their bellies or sides. Lit up like underwater amusement park rides, they swim in large schools, moving with the current. Their lights help them to hide from animals swimming below. When an animal looks up, it doesn't see the fish's shadow. It sees only a weak glow.

A deep-sea worm hides in a yellowish cloud of light. The worm has light-producing organs and pores that contain color pigment on the ends of its many legs. When disturbed, the worm squirts a bioluminescent liquid from each of its leg pores. The liquid completely surrounds the worm or leaves a glowing trail to distract predators while the worm swims away. A thimbleful of the worm's liquid light contains hundreds of tiny rod-shaped capsules of pigment that glow bright yellow.

A DEEP-SEA WORM

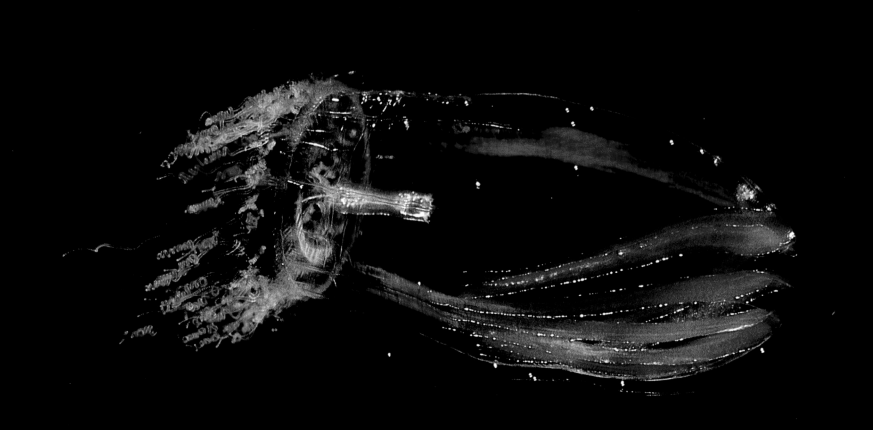

Like tiny spaceships pulsing through the water, jellyfish glitter and shine. Their slippery, squiggly, wiggly bodies are shiny bags of water. They are very fragile. Many jellyfish are bioluminescent. Some of them release clouds of glowing particles into the water to distract or blind an enemy. Some wave their shining tentacles to attract prey.

A GLASS JELLYFISH FROM THE ARCTIC OCEAN

Some sea cucumbers living in the deep ocean have a neat trick. They use their bioluminescence as a burglar alarm. If a predator comes to eat them, they simply shed their glowing skin, which sticks to the predator, marking it as a target for other hunters of the deep.

THIS SHALLOW-WATER SEA CUCUMBER IS MORE BRIGHTLY COLORED THAN ITS DEEP-SEA COUSIN. BUT BOTH HAVE SIMILAR DEFENSE SYSTEMS. WHEN THIS SEA CUCUMBER SENSES DANGER, IT RELEASES LONG WHITE STICKY THREADS.

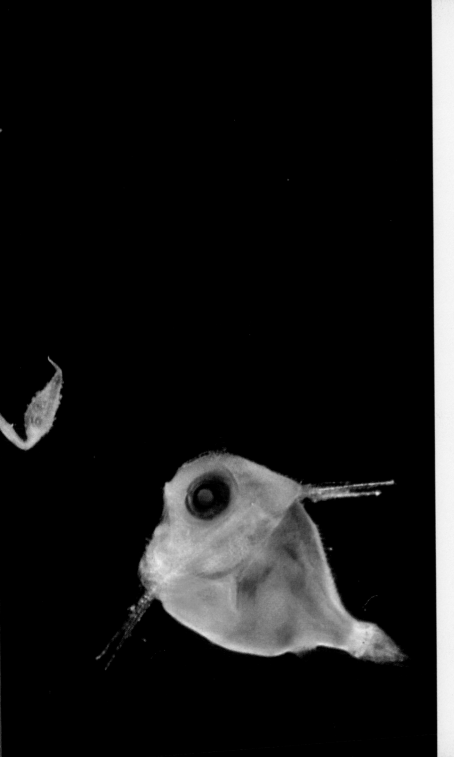

Anglerfish are among the strangest animals in the deep ocean. Females can grow up to twenty times larger than the male. The female anglerfish has a fake fishing rod that grows out of her head. On the end of this rod is a fleshy bulb filled with glowing bioluminescent bacteria. The phony bait looks like a delicious worm to some small fishes. Closer and closer a small fish swims as it tries to catch the bait. Suddenly, the angler's jaws snap shut. Instead of getting a meal, the little fish becomes one.

IN NATURE SOME ANIMALS ARE PREDATORS, OR HUNTERS. OTHER ANIMALS ARE HUNTED. THEY ARE CALLED PREY. THE OCEAN NEEDS BOTH PREDATORS AND PREY TO STAY HEALTHY.

The black dragonfish shimmers and glows with lights along its sides that hide its dark shape. Looking up, a predator would not see the fish's body, only a weak light that is not shaped like a fish.

The female dragonfish, which is eight times larger than the male, has a fake lure dangling from her chin. The phony bait sparkles, tricking smaller fishes into swimming near the huge, toothy mouth that's waiting for dinner.

At least three kinds of dragonfish have red headlights beneath each eye. They are the only known ocean animals that make red light, and only another dragonfish can see it.

THIS DRAGONFISH LIVES DEEP DOWN IN THE OCEAN, FAR FROM THE SURFACE WHERE YOU SWIM.

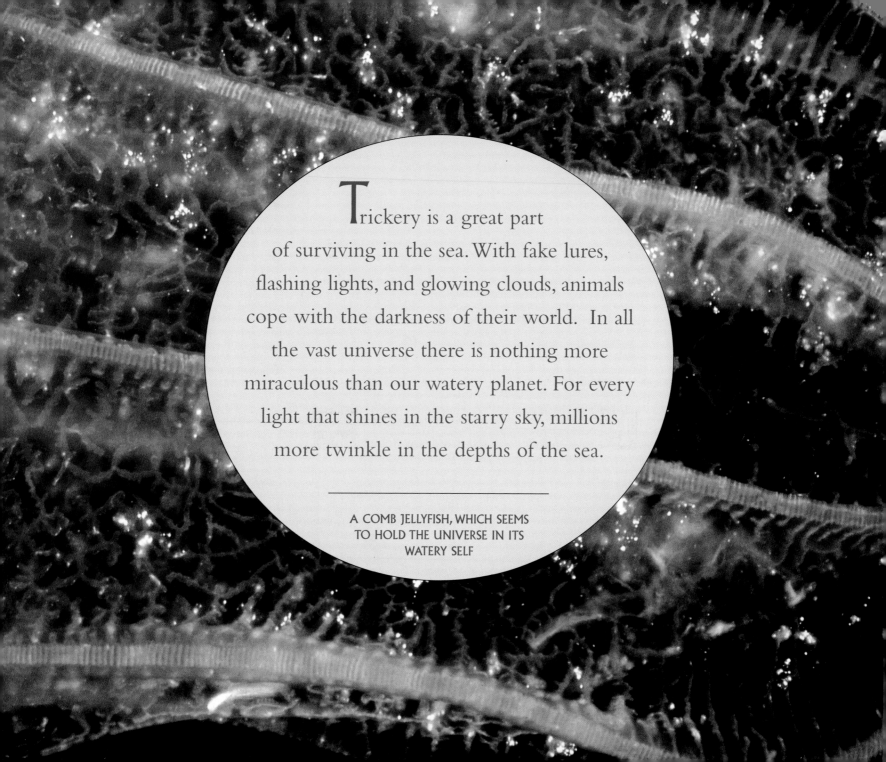

Trickery is a great part
of surviving in the sea. With fake lures,
flashing lights, and glowing clouds, animals
cope with the darkness of their world. In all
the vast universe there is nothing more
miraculous than our watery planet. For every
light that shines in the starry sky, millions
more twinkle in the depths of the sea.

———————————————

A COMB JELLYFISH, WHICH SEEMS
TO HOLD THE UNIVERSE IN ITS
WATERY SELF